"Smile, it's charity."

About the Author

Mishaal Khan

Meet Mishaal, the cybersecurity superhero armed with light-hearted humor! When he's not busy defending digital fortresses, Mishaal is moonlighting as a dad, armed with a repertoire of dad jokes that could make even the toughest hacker crack a smile. From his days as an ethical hacker to his time managing security at corporations, Mishaal has danced through firewalls and juggled more controls than a circus performer. With a knack for translating tech jargon into laughs and an international perspective as diverse as a bag of mismatched USB cables, Mishaal is not just a cybersecurity guru – he's a catalyst for change and a guardian of giggles in the face of digital disaster. So, buckle up, log in, and get ready to LOL your way to better cybersecurity, one dad joke at a time!

1.   Where do hackers go on vacation?

On a phishing trip.

2.   How do pentesters get drunk?

They take screen shots.

3.   Why do infosec people like mummies?

Because they are fully patched.

4.   What did Jay Z say when Rehana got hacked?

I got 99 problems but a breach ain't one.

5.   Why are cybersecurity folks so lonely?

They are afraid of attachments.

6.   What do you call a fat computer?

A big mac.

7.   You can't call a computer fat,

it's not PC.

8. Spiders are the only web developers that enjoy finding bugs.

9. What did one hacker say to the other?

Nothing, they just ransomware.

10. Why do CISOs turn in bed 50 times a night?

Because their turnover rates are very high.

11. What's the best way to catch a runaway robot?

Use a botnet.

12. How did the vegetable farmer sell his produce on the dark web?

He used the onion router.

13. I told my grandfather to pick a password at least eight characters long with one capital.

So, he picked SnowWhiteAndtheSevenDwarvesParis

14. I love the F5 key.

It's just so refreshing.

15. CAPS LOCK: Preventing Logins Since 1980

16. My cousin just got fired from the keyboard factory.

They said he just wasn't putting in enough SHIFTs. They wouldn't even let him RETURN or ENTER. They even changed all the CAPS LOCKs.

17. What did the hacker's out-of-office message say?

Gone phishing.

18. Did you hear about the computer that kept rebooting?

It was terminal.

19. Why can't Lady Gaga use Face ID?

Because it can't read her poker face.

20. So, the other day I started to whisper, and my wife asked why I was whispering.
I told her I didn't want Mark Zuckerberg to hear us.

I laughed.
My wife laughed.
Alexa laughed.
Siri laughed.

21. Why doesn't Superman fight cybercrime?

He's afraid of Krypto Currency!

22. Why does Justin Timberlake love NTP so much?

Because it keeps his systems N Sync

23. Why do InfoSec guys never sit in the center aisle on a plane?

Because they don't want to be the man-in-the-middle

24. Why are hackers not stoners?

Because they pass the hash.

25. What do security analysts clean their floors wit?

Ping sweeps.

26.   What does a baby computer, made in Australia, call its father?

Data

27.   Why do hackers live in basements?

Because they keep breaking Windows

28.   Why are hackers terrible civil engineers?

Because they always build reverse tunnels

29.   The "S" in IOT stands for Security.

30.   What do you call a group of math and science geeks at a party?

Social engineers.

31.   Why do security analysts always stomp on mushrooms?

To prevent Smurf attacks

32.   The recipe called for salting the food.

Now I don't know what I cooked.

33.   What are a CISO's two biggest
cybersecurity fears?

Everyone who works at the
company,
and everyone who doesn't.

34.   I lost all my data once.

But I just asked the NSA for a copy.

35.   The truth is out there.

Anybody got the URL?

36. I found a spider under my computer
the other day.

Turns out he's a web developer. He
works for Amazon Web Services. He
crawled under my keyboard. But
he's under control.

37. Treat your password like
underwear.

Don't show it to strangers,
change it regularly,
and make sure to replace it
immediately if there's a leak.

38. I had a girlfriend but she
ransomware.

Now I WannaCry

39.   What does a hacker do after eating a lot of candy?

Burp Sweet.

40.   The Internet: where men are men, women are men, and children are FBI agents.

41.   Some things Man was never meant to know.

For everything else, there's Google.

42.   Unix is user friendly.

It's just selective about who its friends are.

43. Failure is not an option.

It comes bundled with your Microsoft product.

44. I would love to change the world.

But they won't give me the source code.

45. A TCP packet walks in to a bar and says, "I want a beer."

The barman says, "You want a beer?"
The TCP packet says "yes, a beer."

46.   In high society, TCP is more welcome than UDP.

At least it knows a proper handshake.

47.   I'm not anti-social.

I'm just not user friendly.

48.   A bunch of TCP packets go into a bar, until it's overcrowded.

The next day, half as many go in.

49.   A bunch of TCP packets walk into a
      bar.

      The bartender says, "Hang on just a
      second, I need to close the
      window."

50.   The great thing about TCP jokes is
      that you always get them.

51.   A DHCP packet walks into a bar and
      asks for a beer.

      The bartender says, "here, but I'll
      need that back in an hour!

52.   DHCP jokes only work when there is
      only one person telling them.

53.   I'd make a joke about UDP, but I
      don't know if anyone would get it.

54.   If you want to hear an ICMP joke,
      just ping me.

55.   Person 1: How did you like my HTTP
      200 joke?

      Person 2: It was OK.

56.   What do you call a VPN that isn't
      private?

      A proxymoron

57.   I wanted to post an HTTP joke in
       this thread.

       But I am feeling kind of insecure
       about it.

58.   I tried to come up with an IPv4 joke.

       But the good ones were already
       exhausted.

59.   Astronauts use Linux.

       Because they can't open windows
       in space.

60.   When Chuck Norris uses a password
      manager, it tells him:

      "password not strong enough"
      He types in his name, and it tells
      him *"password too strong"*

61.   Linux isn't magic.

      It's sudo science.

62.   Don't use fortnight as your
      password.

      It's Two Week.

63. I went to an Alzheimer's support forum site.

There was no button to log in, only "I forgot my password."

64. Why did the programmer leave the camping trip early?

There were too many bugs.

65. Why did the hacker send back their breakfast?

Because the restaurant didn't salt their hashes

66. Why was the computer cold?

It left its Windows open.

67. Why do programmers wear glasses?

Because they can't C#

68. What did the programmer say to the barman?

Can I have a byte?

69. Why did the developer go broke?

He used up all his cache.

70. Why did the database admins wife divorce him?

Because he had 1-to-many relationships.

71. Why did the database administrator get kicked out of the bar?

They kept trying to join tables.

72. Why did the IT guy refuse to eat at the diner? They didn't want to deal with all the servers.

73. Why did the computer go to the doctor?

It had a terminal illness.

74. Why do routers hate talking to each other?

Because they always get stuck in a loop!

75. Did you hear, MySpace got hit by a DDOS attack.

More than 8 users were disconnected.

76. Why are fishermen perfect candidates for cybersecurity jobs?

Because they can cast a wide net and catch any phishing attempts.

77. Why did the encryption algorithm feel so secure?

It had a key to happiness, and no one else could decipher it.

78. Why did the IT security manager switch to decaf?

He wanted to minimize the risks of a Java exploit.

79. Why did the security analyst put his laptop in the freezer?

To keep it safe from Spectre and Meltdown.

80. Why do programmers prefer dark mode?

Because light attracts bugs

81. Why did the programmer quit his job?

He didn't get arrays.

82. How do you know if someone is a programmer?

Don't worry, they'll tell you.

83. How many programmers does it take to change a light bulb?

None, that's a hardware problem.

84.   Why did the developer refuse to work on the weekend?

He didn't want to commit to anything.

85.   Why did the software developer go to jail?

He tried to enter an illegal command.

86.   There are 10 types of people in this world.

Those who understand binary and those who don't.

87. The best thing about a Boolean is:

Even if you are wrong, you are only off by a bit.

88. Why did the programmer get lost in the forest?

He didn't know how to branch.

89. Why did the database refuse to get married?

It was already committed.

90. Why did the programmer refuse to watch the TV show "Silicon Valley"?

He said it was too scripted.

91.	Why did the computer cross the road?

	To get to the other subnet.

92.	What do you call a programmer who can't code?

	A project manager.

93.	The oldest computer was owned by Adam and Eve.

	It was an Apple with limited memory; 1 byte and it came crashing down.

94.   I wouldn't worry about your TV and speakers spying on you.

Your vacuum cleaner has been collecting dirt on your for years.

95.   *Girl*: What is your idea of a perfect date?

Programmer: DD/MM/YYYY, other formats can be really confusing.
Girl: You will die single!

96.   My kid called me an old man today.

We both laughed for a while, then I changed the WiFi password.

97.	There are two types of people in this world:

Those who can extrapolate from incomplete data.

98.	A Software tester walks into a coffee shop. Orders a cup of coffee. Orders 0 coffee. Orders 999999999 cups. Orders -1 cups. Orders aktdpos7906.

First real customer walks in and asks where the bathroom is. The coffee shop bursts into flames, killing everyone.

99. What do you need for a good relationship?

Primary Keys

100. They should change the "Mark as read" message on WhatsApp to "Mark has read."

101. I told my doctor that I'm addicted to Instagram.

He said I'm not following you.

102. If 1 out of 10 companies suffered a ransomware attack,
does that mean 9 of them enjoyed it?

103. I once put a band together called 1023 MB.

We never got a gig though.

104. My friend David got his ID stolen last night.

Now I just call him Dav.

105. I saw a great movie about databases today.

I can't wait for the SQL.

106. Did you know that during COVID19 all TCP applications were converted to UDP to avoid handshakes?

107. What's a coders least favorite Pixar
      movie?

      A Bug's Life.

108. WHOIS going to tell us a Domain
      Name joke?

109. Have you heard of the band called
      Dark Web?

      They're always on tor.

110. I have a password joke, it's going to
      crack you up.

111. I changed all my passwords to "incorrect"

So, whenever I forget, it will tell me "Your password is incorrect."

112. What did the motherboard say to her child?

Get on board, you're going to miss the bus.

113. I got an email once on how to read MAPS backwards.

It was SPAM.

114. Why wouldn't TSA let me through airport security?

Because I had bullets in my Word document.

115. Who's the most secure woman in cybersecurity?

Emma Fay (MFA)

116. You know what they say, "age is just a number".

It's actually a string.

117. Why don't hackers hide in forests?

Because there are too many logs to cover their tracks.

118. Why would Darth Vader be such a bad database administrator?

Because he is terrible in sequels.

119. Optimist: The glass is 1/2 full
Pessimist: The glass is 1/2 empty
Excel: The glass is January 2nd

120. I asked a bartender:
What is the WiFi password?

Bartender: You need to buy a drink first

Me: OK, I'll have a Coke

Bartender: Is Pepsi OK?

Me: Sure, how much?

Bartender: $3

Me: Now what's the WiFi password?

Bartender: You need to buy a drink first.

No spaces, all lower case.

121. Someone cracked my password.

Now I need to rename my cat.

122. There are 2 types of tortures for computer nerds in hell.

    1) No matter how many times you flip it, the USB won't go in to your computer.

    2) You must enter your password using a TV remote

123. Did you hear about that tampon company that got breached?

They were quick to stop the bleeding.

124. Why can Winnie the Pooh never get a job in infosec?

Because he keeps stealing the honey pots.

125. I have a GDPR joke, but it's too personal.

126. I have a cybersecurity joke.

But I can't tell you because I'm a gatekeeper.

127. I have a security vendor joke.

I swear I'll deliver it to you before the end of the month.

128. Yo mama so fat, when you download a picture of her at work,

the IT department thinks they're under a DDoS attack.

Index